Jewish Values from Alef to Tav

Joel Lurie Grishaver

Torah Aura Productions
Los Angeles, California

ISBN# 1–891662–62–7

Published by Torah Aura Productions

Torah Aura Productions
4423 Fruitland Avenue, Los Angeles, CA 90058
(800) BE-TORAH • (800) 238–6724 • (323) 585-7312 • fax (323) 585–0327
e-mail <misrad@torahaura.com>
Visit the Torah Aura Website at WW.TORAHAURA.COM

MANUFACTURED IN MALAYSIA

JEWISH VALUES FROM ALEF TO TAV

A VALUE STORY FOR EVERY LETTER OF THE HEBREW ALPHABET

Table of Contents

Emunah

Emunah means faith.
Emunah is believing in God.
Emunah is also knowing
that God believes in you.

The word *amen* comes
from the word *emunah*. Amen means "I can believe that." It is a
way of saying "Me, too." First one person says a whole prayer.
Then a second person hears that prayer and says "amen."
When God hears the "amen" both people get credit for the
prayer.

Sometimes we just say "amen." We see a sunset and say
"amen." We see a painting and say "amen." Sometimes we
listen to a friend or a teacher and say "amen." These are times
of *emunah*.

When Abraham was a boy he was called "Abram." This is a story about Abram. This is not a Torah story. It is a midrash. It is a story that grows out of a Torah story.

Abram Meets God

Long ago Nimrod was a wicked king. Nimrod wanted everyone to bow to him. Nimrod wanted everyone to treat him like a god. Nimrod wanted everyone to believe that he was a god.

One night a huge star came into the sky and ate four other stars. It ate the North Star. It ate the South Star. It ate the East Star. It ate the West Star.

Nimrod asked his wizards, "What does this mean?"

The wizards all said, "A boy has been born who will let people know that you are only a person."

Nimrod said two things. Nimrod first said, "I am a god." Then Nimrod said, "Kill the boy."

For three years they searched for the child. Terah and Amtela were scared. They hid their son Abram in a cave. They wanted him to be safe.

Abram stayed in the cave day and night and looked out at the world. He was lonely. He was scared. He wondered, "Who created the world?" He wondered, "Why am I here?"

Abram saw the sun. The sun was hot. The sun gave light. The sun gave life. Abram thought, "The sun must be god." Then a wind blew a cloud in front of the sun. It got darker. Abram said, "The wind can stop the sun. The wind must be god."

Night came. When the sun went down, the wind stopped. Then the moon rose. Abram said, "The moon must be god." He thought about the moon all night long.

In the morning, the sun rose again. Abram knew that the sun could not be god. Then Abram suddenly knew the truth. He said, "There must be one God who created everything. One God made the sun. The same God made the wind. The same God made the moon. The same God made Nimrod. And the same God made me. I believe in one God."

Then Abram heard a voice that said, "I am here, My son. I believe in you."

Abram said, "I am not alone anymore. I am not afraid anymore." Then Abram said "Amen."

TO THINK ABOUT

1. What did Abram learn in the cave?

2. What is one time when you said "Amen."

3. What do you think is going to happen when Abram and Nimrod meet?

Brit

A *Brit* is a deal between two people. It is a contract. In the Torah a very serious deal is called a "covenant."

We have a brit with God. We are God's partners. God does some things for us. And we do some things for God. There is a *brit* between all people and God. There is a special *brit* between God and the Families-of-Israel.

The Torah is the story of that *brit*.

Noah Was God's Partner

Noah was God's partner. God said to Noah, "I need your help to save the world."

Without Noah, no animal would be alive today. Without Noah, no people would be alive today. Noah helped God save life.

Camels eat straw. Birds eat berries. Monkeys eat bananas. Rabbits like lettuce. Elephants eat branches. Each kind of animal has its own favorite food, but all animals love figs. Feeding all the animals was going to be a lot of work. But that was not the worst thing. This worst thing was that cats eat mice, lions eat cats, and elephants sometimes step on lions because the lions' roar scares them. The ark was very small for so many animals.

God closed the ark's door. The lions roared. The elephants trumpeted. The mice hid. Noah stood on a box. He shouted for quiet. He gathered all the animals. He said, "We are going to make a *brit*. All living things on this ark are going to be partners. Here is the deal. No animal on the ark will eat, hurt, or scare another animal. If you will be good to one another, my family will take care of all of you. No animal needs to be afraid. No animal needs to be hungry. My family will work day and night to feed and take care of everyone."

Every animal said "Yes." Even the lion. Even the mouse. This was the first *brit*. It was the *brit* of the ark.

Noah said, "Dried figs for everyone."

Roosters eat at dawn, while leopards eat at midnight. Giraffes eat in the morning, but cows like to eat three times a day. However, hippopotami eat all the time. Noah's family worked day and night to feed everyone. They fixed all kinds of food. Each pair of animals got the food they liked best, but every animal got dried figs. They all liked the figs. Noah and his family didn't sleep much. They were always tired.

The lions had a problem. They wanted meat. It is very hard for a lion to eat only straw. One day they roared in anger. The roar scared the other animals. Noah picked up a stick and hit a lion. That lion bit Noah on the leg. It was a little bite. Noah walked with a limp from that day on. The lion said, "It is bad enough to make me eat straw. Why do you have to hit me?"

Noah said, "I am sorry."

The lion said, "I am sorry." They forgave each other. The ark was quiet again. This was the *brit*.

Then Noah saw the Urshana bird. It was lying on its side. It looked sick. Noah said, "Urshana bird, what is wrong?"

The Urshana bird said, "You and your family work too hard."

Noah said, "Dear bird, what is wrong with you?"

The bird said, "Nothing is wrong. I have chosen not to eat. That is my way of helping."

Noah brought the bird some figs. He said, "Dear God. The One-who-feeds and sustains everything, please bless this bird with life."

God heard the blessing and said "Yes." That Urshana bird is still alive—somewhere—and will live forever.

The rains stopped. The sun came out. The ark came to rest. God put a rainbow in the sky. God said, "You and I will make a *brit*, too. We will be partners. We will make a deal that the earth will never be destroyed. We will make sure that there are always animals and people. We will make things good. That is our *brit*."

(Bereshit Rabbah 30.6)

17

TO THINK ABOUT

1. Noah and the lion both broke the *brit*. How did they fix it?

2. When we see a rainbow we remember our *brit* with God. What promises are we supposed to remember?

3. When God sees a rainbow God remembers the *brit* with people. What promises is God supposed to remember?

G'milut Hasadim

There are lots of ways of helping other people. You can do it with a smile. You can do it by helping to carry things. You can do it by feeding a hungry person. You can do it by buying food to feed a hungry person.

The Hebrew word for making the world better by giving money is *tzedakah*. The Hebrew words for making the world better by doing the work ourselves are *g'milut hasadim*. It is the way we help other people with our hands, ears, mouths, and especially our hearts.

19

A Visit to Heaven and Hell

Everyone has two angels. One angel collects our good deeds. The other angel collects our sins.

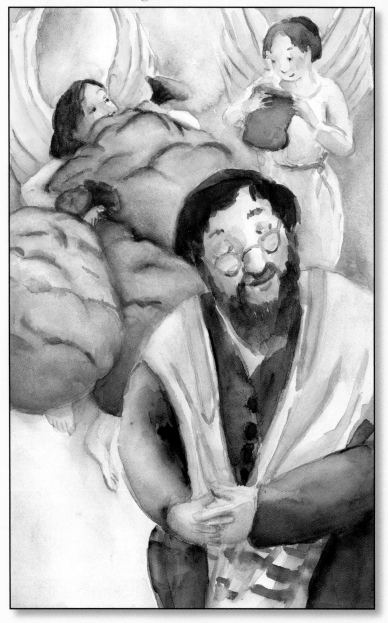

Once there was a rabbi. This rabbi was a totally good person. He did almost nothing wrong. One of the rabbi's angels collected three bags of good deeds. Each bag was heavy. Each bag was full to the top. The other angel who collected sins had an empty bag. There were almost no sins to collect.

The rabbi and his two angels stood in a very long line.

Everyone in the line was going to be judged. The judge would decide if a person went to heaven or if a person went to hell.

The judge saw the rabbi at the end of the line and told everyone else in the line, "Please wait a minute." He walked up to the rabbi. He looked at the three bags of good deeds. He lifted the almost empty bag of sins. He said, "Rabbi, you are a very good man. You are the best person we have seen around here in a long time. We have a very special deal for you. You can visit both heaven and hell."

He said, "Rabbi, you can chose between heaven and hell."

A chariot came and landed by the rabbi. The chariot was on fire but did not burn up. All-white horses pulled the chariot. The rabbi got in. The chariot took off and began to fly. It passed many clouds. After hours and hours it came to a castle floating on a cloud. The chariot stopped.

The drawbridge came down. The door to the castle opened. The rabbi walked across the drawbridge. He went into the great hall. It was filled with many tables. On each table was lots of food. There was every kind of food in the world. It was the best feast ever. The rabbi got hungry.

All of a sudden the rabbi heard the sound of chanting. It was slow and sad. A door opened, and many people entered. They were singing a sad song. They came to the tables, but they could not eat. They were thin and hungry. They were sad. On each person's left hand was tied a giant fork. On the

right hand was tied a giant spoon. They could not bend their elbows. They could not bring food to their mouths.

An angel said, "Rabbi, this is hell. Now go and visit heaven."

He got back in the chariot. It flew and flew again. After hours it came to another castle floating on a cloud. It looked just like the first. The chariot stopped.

The rabbi came into the great hall. It looked just like the first. This great hall was also filled with many tables. On each table was lots of food. There was every kind of food in the world. It was the best feast ever. The rabbi again got hungry.

Again the rabbi heard the sound of chanting. It was happy and glad. A door opened. Many people entered. They were singing a happy song.

They came to the tables. They seemed to be well fed. They were happy. On each person's left hand was tied a giant fork. On the right hand was tied a giant spoon. They could not bend their elbows. The rabbi watched, and they began to eat. Each person picked up food and carried it to his neighbor's

mouth. Here the people fed each other.

The rabbi said, "This is heaven. The people make it heaven. Even though there is no money in heaven, people still found a way to do g'milut _hasadim_."

Then the rabbi said, "I choose to go to hell. I will teach them the secret of creating heaven. That will be my last good deed."

TO THINK ABOUT

1. What made heaven into heaven?

2. Why did the rabbi choose to go to hell?

3. The rabbis said that giving tzedakah was a good thing, but doing *g'milut hasadim* was even better. What makes *g'milut hasadim* better than *tzedakah*?

Derekh Eretz

Derekh eretz is treating someone else with respect.

It is easy to be nice to someone you like. It makes sense to do good things for people who take care of you. *Derekh eretz* is doing nice things for others even if you do not know them. It is doing good things for others even when they have done nothing for you. *Derekh eretz* means doing whatever it takes to make others feel respected.

Rabbi Simon's Jewel

Rabbi Simon ben Sheta<u>h</u> was a poor rabbi. He lived in a time when being a rabbi was not a job. It was a time when being a rabbi was something you did after work.

During the day Rabbi Simon sold cloth. Sometimes he sold it from a little stall in the marketplace. Sometimes he put a big pack on his back and walked from door to door.

During the day he never made much money. After the market closed Rabbi Simon became a teacher. He would teach the words of Torah. In the evening Rabbi Simon was very rich. He had many students who loved him. His students came to him every night but Shabbat to drink in his wisdom. During the day Rabbi Simon was a poor man. At night Rabbi Simon was very rich.

One day Rabbi Simon's students were talking. One said, "Our rabbi works very hard."

Another said, "He is a very good teacher and a very good person."

Another said, "We should help him."

The last student said, "We could buy Rabbi Simon a gift that would help him."

After a lot of talking they decided to buy him a donkey.

One said, "When Rabbi Simon goes to sell his cloth door to door he will not need his big pack anymore."

Another said, "The donkey can carry the cloth for him. He will not be so tired at night."

Another said, "Maybe he will make more money. A donkey can carry more cloth than a old and tired rabbi."

The students went to the marketplace. They made a deal with a non–Jew who was selling a donkey. They looked at the donkey's teeth. They argued about the price. They agreed that the saddle would be included. Finally they had a sale. They shook hands. The non–Jew took the money. The students took the reins and said, "When we move this animal, this donkey and everything on him is ours."

Rabbi Simon loved the gift. He hugged and thanked everyone. He even cried. He said, "I am poor in money but rich in my life."

At the end of the day Rabbi Simon took the saddle off the donkey. Under it he found a jewel. He was amazed. He called his students and asked, "Did you hide this jewel under the saddle?"

They said "No."

"Did you bargain for the jewel?" the rabbi asked.

They said "No."

Then Rabbi Simon asked, "Did the person selling the donkey know the jewel was there?"

The students said, "We made a contract. We said 'When we move this animal, the donkey and everything on him is ours.' You can keep the jewel and never have to work hard again. You can be a rabbi all day long.'"

Rabbi Simon said, "The rules say I can keep the jewel. But that is not the right thing to do. Please take it back to the man who sold the donkey to you."

When the non–Jew who had sold the donkey saw the jewel he started to cry. He said, "Blessed be the God of Rabbi Simon. Blessed be the God of the Jewish people."

That day Rabbi Simon taught his students all about *derekh eretz*. They learned that following the rules is good. They learned that sometimes a Jew needs to do better than the rules. They learned that *derekh eretz* is respecting each person.

Rabbi Simon continued selling and teaching. Rabbi Simon continued working hard by day and being rich by night.

(Jerusalem Talmud, Bava Metzia 2:5)

TO THINK ABOUT

1. Why did Rabbi Simon tell his students to return the jewel when the law said he could keep it?

2. How can one be poor in money but rich in life?

3. How would you explain derekh eretz to a friend?

Havdallah

Shabbat ends when the candle is dipped into the wine. One minute it is Shabbat. The next minute Shabbat is over. The week has started again. At the end of Shabbat we make *havdallah*. *Havdallah* means division. *Havdallah* ends Shabbat. We say a few prayers. We dip the candle in the wine. We divide between Shabbat and the rest of the week.
Jews need to make many divisions.

The Bird in the Hand

This is a story of Ya'akov and his rabbi. Ya'akov was angry at his rabbi.

A rabbi teaches Torah. A rabbi teaches with stories, sermons, and lessons. A rabbi teaches by being a good example. A rabbi is also a judge. A judge is a teacher, too. A judge has to divide between what is right and what is wrong. A judge has to divide between who pays money and who gets money. A judge has to decide who wins and who loses. Judges teach lots of lessons.

At the end of Shabbat we make *havdallah*. *Havdallah* divides the end of Shabbat from the beginning of the week. A rabbi who is a judge makes *havdallah* another way. Here is one such story.

Ya'akov had an argument with his neighbor. He was sure he was right. The two of them asked their rabbi to be the judge. The rabbi said, "Ya'akov, the Torah teaches that your neighbor is right. You have to build him a new chicken coop."

Ya'akov was very, very angry. He thought that the rabbi had been unfair and wanted to get even with her.

One day everyone was in the town square. It was a party. Ya'akov appeared in the middle of the party. He stood at one end of the town square and shouted. He said: "Rabbi, you

are supposed to be smart. Rabbi, you are supposed to be fair. Well, I have a new case I want you to solve. I want you to show the whole town that you are smart. I want you to show everyone that you are a good judge."

Ya'akov held his two hands together. He held them up and showed everyone. He said, "Rabbi, in my hands there is a bird. All I want you to do is tell me one thing. When I open my hands will the bird be dead or alive? Will the dead bird fall to the ground? Will the live bird fly up toward heaven?"

The rabbi thought for a moment, and then she said, "Ya'akov, at the end of Shabbat we make *havdallah*. We divide Shabbat from the week. In *havdallah* there is light and there is shadow. A judge has to make *havdallah*, too. A judge has to divide between what is true and what is not. Today I will be a teacher and you will be the judge. We will make *havdallah* together."

The rabbi took a step closer to Ya'akov. Then she said softly, "The bird in your hands is alive. But if I say that she is alive, you will crush her with your hands and she will die. Then I will be wrong. The bird will be dead. If I tell you that she is dead, you will let her live. You will open your hands and show everyone that I am wrong. Then the bird will fly toward heaven."

There was silence. Then the rabbi took one more step closer to Ya'akov. She said, "You are the judge. Make *havdalah*. Is the bird alive or dead?"

Ya'akov opened his hands. The bird flew toward the sun. It flew up toward heaven. The rabbi said, "Let's dance. Its time to go on with the party. That is my decision."

TO THINK ABOUT

1. What is a *havdallah* service?

2. How does a judge teach?

3. What are times when we must make *havdallah* with our actions.

4. What do you think will happen the next time that Ya'akov talks to the rabbi?

Vikuah

A *vikuah* is an argument. Sometimes people get angry at other people. Sometimes people argue with each other. There are good ways of arguing with each other, and there are bad ways of arguing with each other. It is always better to argue with words. Hitting is almost never a good thing.

There are good reasons to argue, and there are bad reasons to argue. When two students argue over what is true, both of them can learn from that argument. That is a good argument. Jews call it "an argument for heaven." When a person argues just to make another person feel bad, this is a bad argument. Jews call it "an argument not for heaven."

Here are the stories of two arguments. One is "an argument for heaven." One is not.

The Argument Between Moses and Korah

Moses, Aaron and Korah all had the same grandfather. In Egypt Korah was a very rich and important slave. Korah had collected and counted money for Pharaoh. He left Egypt with lots of gold and silver.

God chose Moses and Aaron to lead the Jewish people. Korah was jealous. He was not very important anymore. He said to himself, "I am as important as Moses. I am as important as Aaron. I should be in charge, too."

Korah was looking for a way to be important. One day Moses taught the people the law of the *tallit*. Moses said, "God says every Jew should wear a garment with four corners. On each corner he should tie four threads. Three threads should be white and one should be blue. *Tzitzit* is the Hebrew word for these threads."

Korah said, "I think wearing clothes of all blue is good enough. All blue is better than just four blue threads. I say that anyone in all blue needs no blue threads."

Moses said, "God told us to have *tzitzit*. God said that one should be blue and three should be white."

Korah said, "I was at Mt. Sinai. I heard God tell us to celebrate Shabbat. I heard God tell us not to murder and not to steal. All of us heard God teach the ten commandments. No one but you heard the *tzitzit* law. Moses, I think you made it up. I think you made up most of the laws. You did it so that you could be leader."

Moses said, "God said to wear *tzitzit*. You know what is right."

The next day Korah and 250 followers came to Moses. All of them were dressed in blue. None of them wore *tzitzit*.

Korah said to Moses, "You think you are so important. You think you are so special. You are wrong. God made everyone. You are no better than anyone else. All of Israel is holy."

This began a big argument. It ended badly for Korah. He and all his followers died in an earthquake.

(Midrash Be-Midbar Rabbah 18.1)

39

The Argument Between Hillel and Shammai

Hillel and Shammai were important rabbis. Each of them had a school. Hillel and Shammai never agreed. They agreed on only one thing. They agreed that it was good to argue. The School of Hillel almost always won.

One day the rabbis were deciding the rules for Ḥanukkah. Hillel said, "Light one candle on the first night. Light one more each of the other nights. On the last night you will light eight."

Shammai said, "You've got it backwards. Light eight candles the first night. Light one less each of the other nights. On the last night you will light one."

Hillel asked Shammai, "Why do you think we should count down?"

Shammai answered, "To make it like Sukkot. On Sukkot we bring eight bulls to the Temple on the first night. We then bring seven bulls on the second night. Each night we bring one less. We bring only one on the last night."

Shammai asked Hillel, "And why do you think we should count up to the last night?"

Hillel said, "I think that you should always make things more holy. I think one should never make things less holy. The last night should have the most candles."

The rabbis voted. Hillel won. Today we light our Hannukiyah his way.

After the vote Hillel said to Shammai, "Thank you for teaching me something today." Then Shammai said to Hillel, "Thank you for teaching me something today."

Hillel and Shammai argued a lot. Each argument was a chance to learn something new about the Torah.

TO THINK ABOUT

1. What was wrong about the reason that Korah argued with Moses?

2. What was right about the reason that Hillel and Shammai argued?

3. What is a good reason to argue? What is a bad reason to argue?

ז Z'mirot

Z'mirot is a Hebrew word for songs. Jews like to sing. We sing our prayers. We sing after meals. We sing as families and we sing as a community.

Rabbi Pin<u>h</u>as was the Rebbe of Koretz. He said, "Sometimes one person tries to sing and cannot. Then along comes another person, and they sing together. All of a sudden both of them can sing. The singing connects their souls."

He told the following story.

When Two Sing

Sarah had a beautiful voice. She loved to sing. Sarah sang when she went to the market. Sarah sang when she went out with the sheep. She sang from the top of hills and from the bottom of valleys. She sang with the birds and she sang with the gurgling of the stream. Sarah even sang when she went to sleep at night. People loved Sarah's voice. Everyone who heard her sing became happy.

Then one day Sarah stopped singing. Maybe it was because her family became very poor. Maybe it was because her grandmother was sick. Maybe it was because her best friend Rebekkah moved away. Sarah was now sad all the time. She did not sing anymore. People asked her, "Sarah, why don't you sing?" Sarah would always answer, "I do not know. I just do not feel like it."

The village was now different. The birds still sang. The stream still gurgled. The market was still noisy. Something was missing without Sarah's song.

Sophie had a really bad voice. She could not carry a tune. Sophie liked to sing as much as Sarah did. She sang all the time. But almost every time she did, people asked her to stop singing. People moved away from her when she sang in the market. The sheep started to bleat loudly whenever she sang

near them. It was their way of saying, "Sophie, please stop that noise." The birds flew away when she sang near them. Every night she sang herself to sleep. Every night one of her brothers would shout, "Sophie, stop that noise, we are trying to sleep." Only the stream let her sing. The stream still gurgled when Sophie sang. The stream always gurgled. It did not care.

Sophie went to the forest to sing. No one could hear her there. In the forest Sophie could sing with all her might. She sang with all her heart.

Sarah felt like crying. She was sad and did not want anyone to see her. She did not want anyone to ask about her crying. She did not want to explain. Sarah wanted to cry and not explain. She went to the forest to be alone.

Sarah was walking through the forest. She was crying. Sarah heard Sophie singing. Sophie was way off tune. It did not matter. Sarah decided to sing with her. It was the first time she had sung in a long time. Sophie's voice had lifted her up. The two girls could not see each other. Still they sang together. Sarah's voice helped Sophie stay on tune. Sophie's voice helped Sarah find the joy to sing. They walked toward each other. They kept singing. They sang happy songs and sad songs. They were best friends before they met. From that day on things changed. Whenever Sophie wanted to sing she  found Sarah. Whenever Sarah wanted to sing she found Sophie. The two of them became one voice.

TO THINK ABOUT

1. When are you like Sarah and just don't feel like singing?

2. Are you like Sophie? Is theresomething you love to do that you are not good at doing?

3. When in your life do you feel the magic of two souls connecting and lifting you up?

ח Heshbon ha-Nefesh

Heshbon ha-Nefesh means making a list of the things in our soul. It is a list of our feelings and our actions. Once we have this list the real work begins. Some things must be crossed off. Some things need to move to the top. _Heshbon ha-Nefesh_ is one way Jews work on becoming better people.

49

A Story of Stones

Both men came to the rabbi. Both men wanted to get ready for Yom Kippur. David and Sol both wanted to get rid of their sins.

One time David was angry at his friend. The two friends had an argument. The argument became a fight. The friends yelled at each other. David picked up a stick. He hit his friend. Now he was sorry.

Sol had not hit anyone. He had not stolen anything. He had done no big thing wrong. Sol said to the rabbi, "I have looked at everything I have done. I can find no sins."

The rabbi said to the two men. "I want each of you to do two things. You will be almost forgiven after you do these two things."

Both men said, "I will do whatever you tell me to do."

The rabbi said, "David, I want you to walk across the stream and bring back one big and heavy rock."

David said, "Yes, Rabbi."

The rabbi said to Sol, "I want you to walk across the stream. I want you to pick up as many small stones as you can carry. Then I want you to bring them all back here."

Sol said "Yes" and went to work.

David brought back one big heavy stone and put it at the rabbi's feet. Sol brought a whole armful of stones and put them at the rabbi's feet. Then the rabbi said, "Now is the time for the second job. I want both of you to take your stones back across the stream. David, you must put your stone back where you got it. Sol, I want you to put all of your stones back, too."

David said, "Rabbi, I will do what you say."

Sol said, "There is no way I can do that. I don't remember where I got each stone."

The rabbi said, "Now you are both ready for my lesson. Some sins are big sins. These sins are easy to put back because we remember them. Other sins are very hard to put back because they are hard to remember. We need to work on both kinds of sins."

Both men then said, "Rabbi, will you be our teacher? Will you help us work on our sins?"

TO THINK ABOUT

1. Why should everyone have to make a list of the good things and the problems in his or her life?

2. Name some big sins. Name some little sins. Which are harder to change?

3. If you wrote a _Heshbon ha-Nefesh_ book, what would be the names of some of the chapters?

Teva

Teva is the Hebrew word for nature. It is a mitzvah to guard nature. It is a mitzvah to protect the world. In the beginning God planted a garden in Eden. God asked people to guard it and to keep it. It is our job to guard and keep the world as a garden. This is called *Shmirat ha-Teva*, guarding nature.

Honi Sleeps for Seventy Years

The Land of Israel was filled with trees and bushes. Everywhere you looked it was green. Still Moses told the Families-of-Israel, "Everyone must take a shovel and plant a tree." Moses said, "Just as you found it full of trees, so you must leave it full of trees." Leviticus Rabbah 25.5

Many years passed. The Land of Israel was still very green. It was still filled with trees and bushes. One day Honi the circle-maker was taking a walk. He saw a man planting a carob tree. Honi asked him, "Why are you planting a carob tree in a valley already filled with carob trees?"

The man answered him, "Because I like carobs."

Honi did not like this answer. He then asked in a huff, "Don't you know that it takes seventy years before a carob tree grows fruit? Do you expect to live that long?"

The man calmly said to Honi, "This valley was filled with carob trees when I was born. I want it filled with carob trees when my grandchildren are born. I am planting these trees for them and their friends."

Honi yawned. It was a bright, sunny day, but he felt very tired. He sat down to eat. Then he fell asleep. While he slept a cave formed around him. He slept for seventy years and then awoke. The cave disappeared. He yawned again and opened his eyes. The day was still sunny and bright. Everything looked the same except for one thing. Honi was now sitting in the shade of a beautiful carob tree. He stood up and picked a fruit off it and ate.

Honi saw a man picking fruit off this same tree. He asked the man, "Do you know who planted this tree?"

The man answered proudly, "Of course. My grandfather did. My father and mother planted trees after him. I planted my own trees, and now my children are beginning to plant their own."

Honi said to the man, "May I ask you one more thing?"

The man answered, "Of course."

Honi asked, "May I borrow a shovel?"

Honi, too, planted trees for the future.

Taanit 23a

TO THINK ABOUT:

1. What lesson did <u>H</u>oni learn?

2. If there are already many beautiful trees, why do we have to plant more?

3. Why do we have to guard nature? How else could the mitzvah of guarding the earth be fulfilled?

Yisrael

Yisrael was the name of a man. One night Jacob wrestled with a stranger and got a new name. That new name was *Yisrael*.

Yisrael had a big family. He had twelve sons. His family was called *B'nai Yisrael*, the Family-of-Israel. The family grew and grew and became a nation. This nation was also called *Yisrael*. It is *Am Yisrael*, the People of Israel.

God told Sarah and Abraham to move to a new land. The first name of this land was Canaan. God promised this land to the Jewish people. Its name was changed, too. It, too, became *Yisrael*. It became our land, *Eretz Yisrael*, the Land of Israel.

61

Jacob and the Angels

This is a story that sounds like a Bible story. But it is a midrash, not a Bible story. This story starts in the Torah. It then goes beyond what you will find there.

Jacob grew up in the Land of Canaan. Jacob was not yet called *Yisrael*. The Land of Canaan was not yet called *Yisrael*, either. Jacob decided to leave Canaan when he was seventeen. He went on an adventure to find a wife. One night he slept in a place named Beth El. Jacob used a rock as a pillow. He went to sleep on this rock and had a weird dream. It was a dream of a ladder.

The ladder started at his head. It went all the way up to heaven. Angels were going up the ladder. Angels were coming down the ladder. Angels kept going up. Angels kept coming down. Jacob wondered, "What does this dream mean?"

He asked one of the angels, "Why are you going up the ladder?"

The angel answered, "The land where you are now will become *Eretz Yisrael*, the Land of Israel. I am an angel for *Eretz Yisrael*. This land is different from all the other lands in the world. Now that you are leaving *Eretz Yisrael*, I must leave you."

He asked another angel, "Why are you coming down the ladder?"

The angel said, "I am an angel for the rest of the world. Now that you are leaving *Eretz Yisrael*, I will be the one who goes with you. You can go anywhere in the whole world. You will never be alone. I will be with you until you come back to *Eretz Yisrael*."

In the morning he said, "God was in this place."

Then Jacob went to the birthplace of his mother and father to find a wife. Jacob met his Uncle Laban and married two women. Their names were Leah and Rachel. Jacob and his wives had twelve sons. They also had one daughter. He worked for Uncle Laban for twenty years. At last Jacob was ready to come home.

He packed up the whole family and started back to Canaan. It was a long journey. When the family came to Canaan, the first thing Jacob saw was angels. Jacob said, "These are the Gates of Heaven."

Jacob knew that the angels for outside *Eretz Yisrael* were going up the ladder again. Jacob knew that the angels for *Eretz Yisrael* were coming down the ladder again. Jacob said, "God is everywhere in the whole world. But in *Eretz Yisrael* I am very close to God."

From Rashi on the Two Locations

TO THINK ABOUT

1. What is Jacob's other name?

2. What other things are called Yisrael?

3. How is Eretz Yisrael different from the rest of the world?

כ Kavod

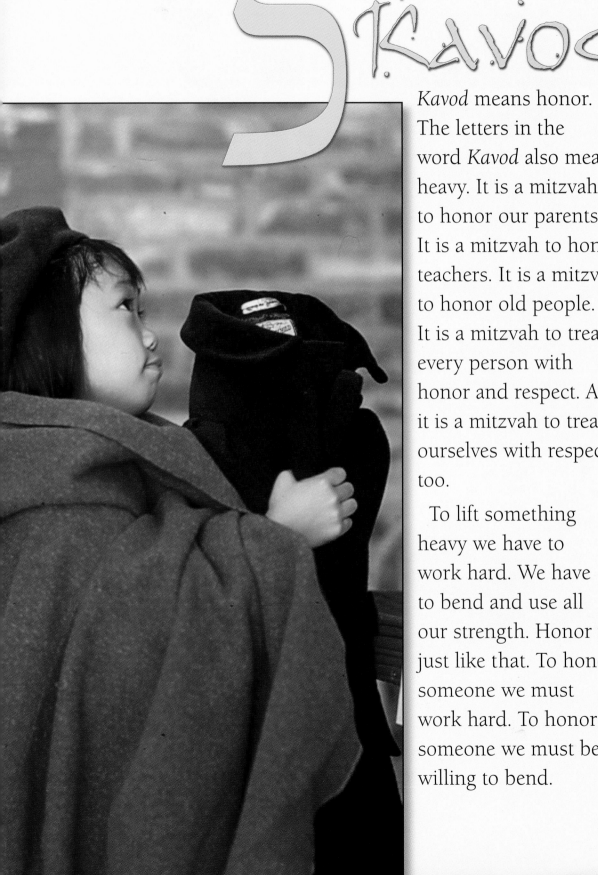

Kavod means honor. The letters in the word *Kavod* also mean heavy. It is a mitzvah to honor our parents. It is a mitzvah to honor teachers. It is a mitzvah to honor old people. It is a mitzvah to treat every person with honor and respect. And it is a mitzvah to treat ourselves with respect, too.

To lift something heavy we have to work hard. We have to bend and use all our strength. Honor is just like that. To honor someone we must work hard. To honor someone we must be willing to bend.

The Wooden Bowl

This is the story of a grandfather, a father, and a son. Father was the son of Grandfather. Son was the grandson of Grandfather. This is a story of their family.

Grandfather started a business when he was young. The business made lots of money. Grandfather was a rich man. Father worked in Grandfather's business. The business made everyone in the family rich.

One day Grandfather said to Father, "I am getting to be old. Right now I want to give everything I own to you. I want you to have my big house. I want you to run the business. I ask only one thing. I want you to take care of me in my old age."

Father took over the business. He paid himself a bigger salary. Father, Son, and the whole family moved into Grandfather's big house. They took over. They also took care of Grandfather. Grandfather got older and older. He needed more and more care. The family got richer and richer. Someone had to sit next to Grandfather at every meal and feed him. Someone had to lift the spoon to Grandfather's mouth. Someone had to wipe the food from Grandfather's chin. Grandfather was now a lot like a child.

One day Father came home from the business. He was tired. He had worked hard. When they sat down to eat Father did not want to feed his father. Father said to Grandfather, "If you want to live in this house, old man, you must feed yourself."

Grandfather picked up the spoon. He tried to lift the food to his mouth. Much food fell on the table. Food was all over Grandfather's face. Father said, "Grandfather, you are eating like an animal."

Father took a wooden bowl. He put Grandfather's dinner in the bowl. He put the bowl on the floor. He helped Grandfather to the floor and said, "You might as well eat like a dog."

In the middle of the night Father woke up. He heard a scratching. He tried to go back to sleep, but all he heard was the scratching. He went looking for the sound. It was not in his bedroom. It was not in the kitchen. It was not even in the room Son and Grandfather shared. Father went out to the porch. He saw his son sitting on a step. Son had a knife and a block of wood. He was carving. The carving made the scratching sound. Father said, "Son, what are you doing?"

The son said, "I am carving a wooden bowl for when you get old."

TO THINK ABOUT

1. Why was Father mean to Grandfather?

2. What do you think happened the day after this story ends?

3. How does this story show why "honor" and "heavy" come from the same Hebrew word?

Lashon ha-Ra

Lashon ha-Ra is Hebrew for "an evil tongue." It teaches that some of the words we speak with our tongues can do harm.

Sometimes our tongues speak words that help people. Some of our words feel like hugs or handshakes. Sometimes words can make us feel better. We speak words that help others. We speak words that do good.

Other words can hurt people. They feel like a slap or worse. When you hit someone in the face it sometimes turns red. You can also speak words that make someone turn red. The rabbis of the Talmud saw people with red faces and taught, "Words can wound." They also said, "Sometimes our tongues are weapons for doing evil." Jews never want to hurt anyone. Not with their hands and not with their words.

The Feather Story

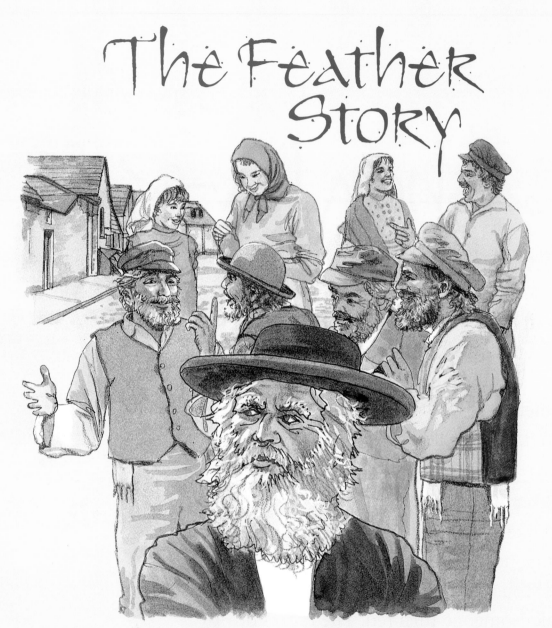

The rabbi was very angry. Everywhere he went it was the same thing. All he heard was laughing. All over town people were whispering and laughing—and the rabbi was getting angrier and angrier. He knew that Nathan was at home crying.

Nathan had done a foolish thing. Barukh had watched and laughed and then told Golda and Fruma about the foolish thing that Nathan had done. They, too, laughed. Fruma told Tevya, Yosi, and Dan, who also laughed at Nathan's foolishness. Yosi told Sarah, who told Benjamin, who told Peninnah. All of them were laughing. Meanwhile, Golda had told her mother, who told her best friend, who told her husband, who told everyone in his store of Nathan's foolish act. Everyone in the store laughed. All over town people were laughing, and they passed along the story of the foolish thing Nathan had done. Meanwhile, Nathan was at home crying.

That night the rabbi heard a knock at his door. It was Barukh.

Barukh said, "I don't know what to do. Nathan won't talk to me. He used to be my best friend. Now he slams the door in my face. All he says is, 'You hurt me.' I said I was sorry, but he wouldn't listen. All he would say was, 'You hurt me.'"

The rabbi understood. He had a plan. He told Barukh, "Meet me tomorrow at noon at the very top of the town clock tower. There I will

teach you a great secret. But you must do one thing. You must bring a pillow with you. Without a pillow I can't teach you anything." Barukh was confused. He didn't understand. But he knew that he had to follow the rabbi's instructions.

At noon they met at the top of the clock tower. They looked down over the whole village. The rabbi told Barukh to rip the pillow open. As soon as he began to tear the pillow the wind began to grab the feathers and carry them away. The rabbi took the pillow out of Barukh's hands. He shook it. The air was filled with feathers.

The wind carried them all over town. They blew into the marketplace and past the school windows. They blew into the backyards and onto the porch outside Golda's mother's best friend's husband's store. Everywhere. The whole town was filled with feathers.

The rabbi then said, "Go and gather up all the feathers."

Barukh answered, "But—that's impossible! No one could do that."

Then the rabbi said, "Then go and gather up the story about the foolish thing that Nathan did."

"But—that's impossible! No one could do that."

Barukh was silent. He thought. Then, finally, he said, "I understand."

TO THINK ABOUT

1. What do you think Nathan did?

2. What lesson did the rabbi teach Barukh?

3. How do the pillow and the feathers teach us about *Lashon ha-Ra*?

Mitzvot

When Adam and Eve were in the Garden of Eden, God gave them one *mitzvah*. It was the command not to eat from the tree in the middle of the Garden. When Noah and his family left the Ark, God gave them seven *mitzvot*. These were commands about how people should live. In the Torah that God gave Israel there are 613 commandments. Jews live by these *mitzvot*. We do our best to keep all of them.

Moses Wins the Torah

A midrash. Moses climbed up to the top of Mt. Sinai. When he got there he saw a ladder. He climbed up and up on the ladder. He went through cloud after cloud. He came to a door in the bottom of the cloud. It said on it, "Trapdoor to the space under God's throne." Moses opened the door. He began to climb up. He stuck his head up. He had to duck quickly. Someone had thrown a shoe at him. He stuck his head up again but had to duck again. A firebomb exploded in his face. Every time he tried to get up something else was thrown or something else exploded.

Moses did not know what to do. Then he had an idea. He took his staff and tied his scarf around it. It looked like a head. He stuck it up through the door. It got hit with all kinds of things. All kinds of firebombs exploded around it. Finally it was quiet. Everything that could be thrown had been thrown. Everything that could explode had exploded. Moses pushed himself up through the hole. He was standing at the bottom of a giant chair. The seat of the chair disappeared in the clouds. All around him were angels standing in a circle. Above him the seraphim and the cherubim and the ofanim and the other heavenly creatures were circling overhead. All of them were

shouting, "Do not give the Torah to Israel. Israel will break the Torah. Keep the Torah in heaven."

Moses wanted to get the Torah for Israel. He said to the angels, "Let's make a deal." He said, "Let me ask you just three questions. After that either you can give me the Torah for Israel or I will quietly climb back down the ladder."

The angels said, "Ask away."

Moses said, "I want all the angels who have ever been disrespectful to their parents to raise their hands." All the angels in heaven grabbed their wrists and said, "Not I. Not once. Never." Then one angel explained, "Angels don't have parents."

Then Moses said, "I want all the angels who have ever stolen anything to shout 'Yo'." All the angels in heaven threw their hands over their mouths. Talking through their fingers they answered, "Not I. Not once. Never."

Then they all said, with their hands still in place, "Angels don't need anything. Angels don't steal."

Finally Moses said, "I want every angel in heaven who has ever murdered anyone to take one step forward." All the angels in heaven took one step back. They wanted to make sure that no one would misunderstand. They all said together, "Never. Don't even think that. Angels don't murder."

Moses said, "That is the point. Only people are disrespectful. Only people steal. Only people murder. The Torah teaches us not to do those things. The Torah gives us the mitzvot we need. People need the Torah, not angels. People need the mitzvot in the Torah to become better people. People need the mitzvot in the Torah to make the world more like heaven."

The angels all agreed. They carried Moses on their shoulders. It became a parade. They put him down by the ladder and gave him the Torah to take back to earth.

Shabbat 88b

TO THINK ABOUT

1. Why did the angels want to keep the Torah in heaven?

2. How did Moses convince the angels that people should get the Torah?

3. How do *mitzvot* help to make us better people? How do help to make the world a better place?

‫נ‬Neshamah

Neshamah is the Hebrew word for the soul.

The Torah tells that God made Adam out of the soil of the earth. God then breathed the breath of life into Adam. Adam came alive. The midrash tells that Moses died as a very old man when God kissed him. God's kiss took away his breath of life.

Our soul is the breath of God that gives us life. It comes into us when we are born. It will return to God when we die. Every person has a different *neshamah*. Every person is different.

85

The King's Orchard

Rabbi Yehudah told this story.

Once there was a king. This king had an orchard. The fruit in that orchard was very sweet. Everyone in the kingdom wanted to eat that fruit. However, no one could ever eat any of it because the king would never let anyone taste it. The king always protected his orchard.

One day the king hired two men to be guards for his orchard. One of the men was blind. One of the men was lame. The king said, "You two are perfect guards. A blind man cannot see my fruit. A man cannot steal what he cannot see. A lame man cannot walk or stand. He cannot reach my fruit. A man cannot steal what he cannot reach. I want you two to make sure that no one eats my fruit. And I do not want either of you to take any of my fruit for yourselves. That is your job."

As soon as the king left, the blind man spoke:

"If we work together, we can steal the king blind. Here is what we are going to do. You are going to climb on my shoulders. You will be my eyes. I will be your legs. Together we will be able to steal lots of fruit. Together we will be able to eat from the king's orchard."

The two men worked together. They ate lots of fruit. They stole lots of fruit.

The king returned and saw how much fruit was missing. The blind man said, "I didn't take it. I am blind and could not see the fruit." The lame man said, "I didn't take it. I am lame and could not reach it."

The king said, "My fruit is missing." Then he figured it out. He told the lame man to climb on the blind man's back. The king said to the blind man, "You are not guilty alone." Then the king said to the lame man, "You are not guilty alone." The he said to the two of them, "But you two are guilty together."

Rabbi Yehudah said, "Our body and our soul are just like the blind man and the lame man. The body says, "I did not eat too much and become fat. It was not me who loves food." And the soul says, "I am not the fat one. It wasn't my hand and my mouth." The body says, "I was not angry with my sister. It was not my idea to slap her." And the soul says, "It wasn't my hand on her cheek."

God turns to us and says, "You are you. Your body and your soul are a team. You are responsible for everything you do. There is no one else to blame."

Sanhedrin 91a

TO THINK ABOUT

1. What job did the king ask the blind man and the lame man to do? Why did the king think they would be good at it?

2. How did the blind man and the lame man cheat the king?

3. How are your body and your soul like the blind man and the lame man?

ד Siddur

The alphabet has an order. It is A, then B, then C. Numbers also have an order. Numbers go 1, then 2, then 3. Seder is the Hebrew word for order.

Siddur is the Hebrew name given to the prayer book. It comes from the word *seder*. It is called a *siddur* because it gives us the order of the prayers said at every service. Jewish services are like the alphabet and like numbers. Jewish services always go in the same order.

91

The Horse Who Could Pray

Everyone heard the shouting. There were lots of people in the synagogue. It was almost full. Everyone was waiting for the service to begin. Then the shouting began. It came from the back. Everyone turned to look.

One man shouted, "I'll bet you ten kopeck you can't."

The stranger shouted, "I'll bet you ten kopeck I can."

A third man shouted, "Five more kopeck says you can't."

Then the rabbi walked in and asked, "What is going on here?"

The first man said, "This man says he can teach my horse to pray. He says that he can make him pray just like any other Jew. I bet him he can't."

Seven different men said, "So did I."

The rabbi said, "A praying horse is something I would like to see. It might teach all of you something."

The stranger took the horse. He went away for a month. Then the day came. He and the horse were standing in the back of the synagogue. Everyone else was standing, too. There was no room to sit. Everyone in the whole town was there. Everyone from miles away was there, too. Everyone wanted to see the horse that could pray.

The stranger picked up a huge *siddur*. He held it up for everyone to see. He said, "I have taught this horse the *seder* of the service." The stranger took the *siddur* and placed it on the shtandard. A shtandard is the desk that some Jews use as a table to hold books when they pray or study. He put a kippah and a tallit on the horse.

Someone joked, "Now the horse looks like a Jew. But can he pray like a Jew?"

The horse went over to the shtandard. He looked in the *siddur*. He bowed his head up and down, up and down. After a little while he put his nose into the *siddur* and turned the page. Then he did it again and again. The horse's head went up

94

and down, up and down. Then the horse turned the page. He looked just like a Jew who was really praying.

The man said, "I have won the bet."

The rabbi walked over and patted the horse. Then he walked over to the shtandard. He picked up the *siddur* and shook it. Oats, lots of oats, fell out of the pages. Everyone in the synagogue laughed.

The rabbi said, "Don't laugh so hard. The horse

prays the way most of you do. The horse knows how to turn the pages. The horse knows how to follow the order. But the horse does not know how to mean his prayers. Still, the horse does pray better than some of you."

Everyone in the synagogue laughed.

TO THINK ABOUT

1. Why do Jews call their prayerbook a *siddur*?

2. Did the stranger win or lose the bet?

3. What does it take to really mean a prayer?

Aseret ha-Dibrot

God created the world by speaking only ten sentences. Theses ten sentences are called the "ten times God spoke."

At Mount Sinai God spoke to all of Israel. God taught the ten rules. These rules are called the *Aseret ha-Dibrot*. The Hebrew actually means "The ten things that God said."

God created the world so that people could learn to live by God's rules.

Moses Drops the Ten Commandments

Six hundred thousand Israelites came to Mount Sinai. All of them were gathered at the foot of the mountain. They were ready to meet their God. They spent three days getting ready. Six hundred thousand of them had taken a bath. Six hundred thousand of them were wearing clean clothes. All of them were standing there with clean hearts.

Mount Sinai began to smoke. A loud shofar sounded.

A ball of fire came down from the heavens and landed on top of the mountaintop. The top of the mountain was on fire. The whole mountain shook—a lot. The sound of the shofar got louder and louder. It was awesome. God told Moses not to let the people come too close.

God taught the Ten Commandments to the people. "I am your God. Do not make idols. Do not tell lies and swear by My name. Remember Shabbat. Honor your parents. Do not murder. Be true to your husband or wife. Do not steal. Do not lie in court. Do not wish to have anything that belongs to your neighbor."

When God spoke to Israel at Mount Sinai it was a miracle. People saw the sound of the lightning. People saw the sound of the shofar. Everyone was impressed. Everyone was scared. All six hundred thousand people took a few steps backwards. They said to Moses, "You talk to God for us, and we will listen to you."

Moses went up to the top of the mountain. He spent forty days and forty nights there. God taught him Torah. God also carved the Ten Commandments into two tablets of stone. The tablets were very heavy. They were also very holy.

God carved the letters all the way through the stone. The letters worked with God's power.

The letter ס, *samekh*, in Hebrew looks a lot like the letter "O" in English. If you cut the middle out of an "O" it will not stay in place. When God carved the *samekh* the middle of the *samekh* stayed in the middle of the letter.

If you cut a letter ע Ayin out of a sheet of paper, it will look good on one side. It will look backwards on the other side. The letters on the Ten Commandments were carved with God's power. They looked perfect on both sides.

Moses was gone a long, long time. The people were worried that he was not coming back. They were worried that God had left them. They made an idol to be a new god. They made an idol of a calf out of gold.

The tablets of the Ten Commandments were too heavy for any person to carry. But Moses easily picked them up. This, too, was part of the power of the letters. The letters God carved lifted the stones. Moses took the tablets and went down the mountain. It was easy. The tablets almost carried him.

When Moses came close to the camp he saw the Golden Calf. He saw the people dancing and singing and worshiping this idol. He knew that Israel was in trouble. The tablets in his hands said "No idols." There was Israel worshiping an idol. He knew that God would punish them for breaking the rules in his hand. He sighed a deep sigh. Before he could do anything, a letter flew out of the stone and whispered, "We will help." Then, like a flock of birds taking off together, the letters flew off the stones. The tablets became too heavy for Moses to hold. They fell to the ground with a crash.

Israel got a second chance. Moses destroyed the calf. Then God made him go up the mountain and carve a second set of tablets. Israel got to start over.

Portions of Exodus 20-24, selections of Midrash, including the Talmud, Shabbat 104.

TO THINK ABOUT

1. What was it like to be at Mount Sinai when God spoke to Israel? What could one see or hear?

2. What was special about the tablets and the carving of the Ten Commandments?

3. God gave Israel 613 *mitzvot* (commandments). What makes these ten rules so important?

Pikuah Nefesh

In the Torah God tells us to "choose life." Sometimes we must make a choice. There are times we must choose between doing something Jewish and keeping someone alive. At those times God wants us to "choose life." Sometimes we have to choose between obeying some rule found in the Torah and saving some person's life. At those times God wants us to "choose life." Life is holy. Life is a gift from God. *Pikuah Nefesh* is the name of the mitzvah to "choose life."

Hillel is Frozen

Once there were two brothers. They lived in Babylon. One brother was named Hillel. The other brother was named Shevna. Shevna spent all of his time on business. He became very rich. Hillel put all of his time into the study of Torah. He became very smart and very learned. He was also very poor. Shevna told his brother that he was very foolish to spend all of his time on Torah. He said, "You should first earn a decent living and then study Torah in your spare time."

Hillel said, "Brother, you do not understand. You have not learned that the Torah is life."

Hillel studied and studied. He learned much. Still he had three questions that no one in Babylon could answer. There were teachers in Jerusalem who knew more Torah than anyone in Babylon.

Hillel owned few things. His best clothes were not very good. More and more Hillel wanted to know the answer to his three questions. One day he packed the best of his clothes and a few of his few things into bag. He began the long walk from Babylon to Israel. After a very long journey Hillel came to Jerusalem. He had no money left.

The best teachers in Jerusalem were Shemayyah and Avtalion. They charged money to study in their school. Hillel was

very modest. He was embarrassed that he had three questions that he could not answer. He told no one how much he knew. Instead he got a very basic job. Hillel earned only two coins a day. He needed one coin to pay for food and a place to live. He needed the other coin to pay the gatekeeper to let him into the school.

One Thursday afternoon Hillel's boss told him that there was no work. Hillel had no way of earning money. He had no money in his purse, either. That night he went hungry. The next morning he went to the school but had no money to pay. The gatekeeper would not let him in. Hillel was sad. Then he had an idea. He sneaked up on the roof. Over the classroom there was a skylight with metal bars. He lay down over the bars and listened to the class. It was winter. It began to snow. Hillel was cold. Hillel was hungry. He fell asleep. The snow covered him.

Shabbat morning the students and the teachers came into the school for Shabbat services. The room was very dark. They looked up at the skylight and saw the shape of a person. They ran up on the roof. They found Hillel and brought him inside. He was frozen. They rubbed his whole body.

One student said, "He needs the warmth of a fire in order to live, but the Torah says we cannot light a fire on Shabbat."

Shemayyah and Avtalion said, "Light the fire. We must choose life. We must break this rule about Shabbat so that Hillel can live to celebrate many more Shabbatot."

When Hillel woke up his first words were, "The

Torah is life." Soon Hillel became one of the most famous Jewish teachers of all time.

Talmud, Yoma 35b

TO THINK ABOUT

1. When should a Jew break a Jewish law or Jewish custom to do *pikua<u>h</u> nefesh*?

2. Can you think of times when a Jew should not do *pikuah nefesh*?

3. What does it mean when we say that "The Torah is life"?

צ

Tzedakah

Jews have many words for helping to make the world better. Each of these words teaches a different lesson.

G'milut hasadim are two words with one lesson. We should help others because God loves us. We do the same things for other people that God does for us. We comfort them. We feed them. We heal them. We help them in all kinds of ways.

Tzedakah is a word with two lessons. One lesson is that we can use our money to do *g'milut hasadim*. We can buy food, pay rent, and hire helpers. Our money can make sure that good deeds happen. The other lesson is found in the word *tzedakah*. *Tzedakah* is built out of the word *tzedek*. *Tzedek* means "justice." The lesson we learn is that *tzedakah* is an act of justice. It is something we have to do. *Tzedakah* is more than a favor or a good deed.

The Rich Man and the Mirror

Everyone called her "The Rebbetzin." That was the only name
people knew anymore. Her husband had once been the rabbi
in town. He was now long dead. The town had a new rabbi.

He had a wife who was his rebbetzin. The new rebbetzin was a wonderful woman who did many *mitzvot*. Still, everyone called Golda "The Rebbetzin." She visited the sick. She fed the hungry. She taught the children. But most of all she collected *tzedakah*. At night she sat with the other women and studied the holy books.

In town there was a very rich man. He lived in a big house. He dressed in fancy clothes. He had the best of everything. This rich man kept everything for himself. He gave no money to *tzedakah*. He spent no time doing *g'milut hasadim*. The rich man was alone all the time. He was mean to no one. All he did was take care of himself.

One day "The Rebbetzin" knocked on the rich man's door. She told him, "There is a family in this town who needs your help. The roof of their house is leaking. The father of this family is sick in bed. They have no wood to put in their stove. The children are crying because they are hungry. The mother sits quietly because she has no way of fixing any of these things. All their money is gone. I need you to give a few coins to help them."

The rich man said to "The Rebbetzin," "Your way is not my way. I am not like you. I do not want to give my money away."

He started to shut the door. "The Rebbetzin" held the door. She walked into his house. She looked at a mirror.

The rich man said, "This is a very famous mirror. It once belonged to a Queen of France."

She said to the rich man, "Please look in the mirror. Tell me what you see."

The man walked to the mirror. He looked into the glass and said, "I see myself."

She then walked to the window and said, "Please come over here. Please tell me what you see."

The man walked to the window. He looked out of the glass and said, "I see the street. I see the boy playing with his ball. I see the girls jumping rope. I see the old man walking on his cane."

"The Rebbetzin" said to him, "The mirror is a sheet of glass. The window is a sheet of glass. There is just one difference. When you cover the glass with silver all you can see is yourself. People are like that, too. When you cover them with silver all they can see is themselves."

The rich man looked at her and smiled.

This story is a Jewish folktale

TO THINK ABOUT

1. What is the difference between *tzedakah* and *g'milut <u>h</u>asadim*?

2. What kind of things did the old rebbetzin do with her time?

3. Why do you think the people of the town called her "The Rebbetzin" even though there was a new rebbetzin?

4. How do you think this story ends? What do you think the rich man did next?

רKedushah

God created people *b'Tzelem Elohim*. *B'Tzelem Elohim* means "in the image of God." It does not mean that people look like God. It does means that people are able to act like God.

In the Torah God tells people, "You shall be holy because I am holy." We learn that God is holy and people can be holy if we act like God. Acting like God means feeding the poor, being fair in business, making sure that courts are just, and treating every person with respect. When we live *b'Tzelem Elohim* we can be holy. *Kedushah* is the Hebrew word for holiness.

Levi Kelman Sees God

It was Sukkot or maybe it was Shavuot. It was a morning when services were long. And it was one of those holidays when the Kohanim blessed the congregation. Levi Kelman was six or maybe seven or maybe even eight yeard old. He had been sitting in services a long time. He did not want to sit much longer. All of the people who were named Cohen or Kahn were called to the bimah. These were families who remembered that their relatives had been Priests in the time of the Temple. These Kohanim were going to bless the congregation. Levi's father called him over. His father tried to wrap Levi in the huge tallit he wore. He wanted to hide Levi's eyes. Levi did not want to stand still. He asked his father, "Why can't I look at the Kohanim?" His father said in a whisper, "Because when the Kohanim say their blessing, God appears between their fingers."

In a big voice Levi said, "I have a question. I thought God was invisible. Why can't I look?"

His father said, "Shush." Then he said, "Come over here." Then he added, "Quietly."

Levi continued in his big voice, "I have another question. Can God see God? God is invisible, but God is also supposed to see everything. When God looks at God, can God see God?"

His father gave him a simple answer. "Shush, Levi, this is a service!" Then his father said, "Get over here."

Wolfe Kelman wrapped his son in his big tallit. He held him in a soft, warm hug during the blessing of the Kohanim. When this was all done, Levi again asked his father, "Can God see God?"

This time his father turned to Levi and said, "Why don't you go and ask your question to Dr. Heschel?"

Abraham Joshua Heschel was a philosopher. He was a famous Jewish teacher. He sat on the opposite side of the synagogue from the Kelmans. Levi walked across the whole synagogue. He walked up to Dr. Heschel. He pulled on his tallit. Then Levi said politely, "Dr. Heschel, I have a question. My father said I should ask you."

Dr. Heschel said, "Levi, what is your question?"

Levi asked his question. "Can God see God?"

Dr. Heschel said, "Levi, this is a wonderful question. It is like other great Jewish questions. Can God think of a thought God has never thought of before? Can God make a rock so big that God cannot move it?"

Levi almost shouted, "But can God see God?"

Dr. Heschel turned to him and said, "Shush, Levi, this is a service."

More than a week passed. Levi was getting ready for bed. His father walked into the room. He was smiling. He said, "Levi, do you remember the big question you asked in services?"

Levi smiled. He nodded his head.

His father said, "Son, I have been thinking and thinking and now I have an answer." Then he said, "When you want to see yourself, where do you look?"

Levi answered quickly, "In a mirror."

His father smiled. Then he said, "Well, when God wants to see God, God looks at you."

There was a funny look on Levi's face. Then his father said. "God looks at you, to see if God can see God in the things you do."

Levi smiled. He was even silent for a minute or two.

From a true story

TO THINK ABOUT

1. Why did Wolfe Kelman try to hide his son's eyes during the blessing part of the service? Do you think that God really appears between the fingers of the Kohanim?

2. What did Levi ask his father and Dr. Heschel?

3. When do you do things that will let God see God?

4. What does it mean to be *b'Tzelem Elohim*?

Rodef Shalom

Shalom is a Hebrew word I bet you know. It means hello and good-bye. It also means peace. The word *rodef* means "a person who chases." In the Talmud we are taught that peace doesn't just happen. People have to make peace. People have to chase peace. Peace is not automatic. The midrash even says that God once told a lie to Abraham so that there would be peace. Making peace is another way to be like God.

121

Rabbi Meir Makes Peace

Rabbi Meir was a great teacher. Every Friday afternoon he would teach a class that anyone could attend. Both men and women came to this class. He would teach things he learned from the Torah. He would teach things he learned from his teachers. Sometimes he taught things he learned from his mother. In one class he said, "My mother taught me this. Sometimes the best way to fix a sore eye is to spit in it." Every student in class laughed.

One woman came to Rabbi Meir's class week after week. She loved to study. She thought he was the best teacher. Often she came home late. Sometimes she did not get the Shabbat dinner ready in time. One week she came home very late. Almost nothing was ready for Shabbat. Her husband came home. He saw that the table was not ready. He saw that dinner was not going to be ready for a long time. His children jumped on him. They had not been washed. They were not dressed in Shabbat clothes. He became very angry. He screamed at his wife, "Where is Shabbat in this house?"

She said, "Please help me. We will make Shabbat together. I am late because I stayed at Rabbi Meir's class."

This was a week when her husband was too angry. He said words that he later hated. He said, "You think that Rabbi Meir

is more important than your family. You like him more than you like me. You spend more time with him than you do with us. Get out of this house. Do not come back until you have spit in Rabbi Meir's face."

The woman ran from the house. She was crying.

Rabbi Meir was in the synagogue. He was getting ready for Shabbat. While he was sitting alone the door opened. It was Elijah. Elijah is the prophet who never died. Elijah is the prophet who helps God. Elijah told the rabbi about the woman and her husband. The rabbi learned all about their Shabbat argument.

Elijah left. The door to the synagogue opened again. The woman came in. She was crying. She wiped her face quickly. She sat in a corner far away from Rabbi Meir. Rabbi Meir began to blink and blink. He looked up at the ceiling. He put his hand on and off his right eye. He moaned a little bit. He blinked and blinked. He put his hand on and off his eye. He moaned some more.

The woman walked over. She said, "Rabbi, what is wrong?"

He said, "My eye is sore. I have prayed for help. But nothing seems to make it better."

The woman said, "Don't you remember what your mother told you? You told it to us. Sometimes the best way to fix a sore eye is to spit in it."

The Rabbi said, "But who could I ask to spit in my eye?"

The woman said, "I would do it for you."

She spat in the rabbi's face. He smiled. He said, "Thank you." And then he said, "Now go home and make Shabbat with your family."

She left, and the rabbi took out his handkerchief and wiped his face. He laughed a big laugh. He said to himself, "Sometimes making peace is a lot of work."

The woman came home. She found her husband in an apron working in the kitchen. It was almost ready for Shabbat. He said, "Shabbat is almost here."

She said, "I have done what you said. I have spat in Rabbi Meir's face." Then she took the broom and said, "You make sure the kids are ready. I will finish in here." They kissed each other and said, "*Shabbat Shalom*."

Deuteronomy Rabbah 5.15

TO THINK ABOUT

1. Why was the woman's husband angry?

2. Why did he get too angry?

3. How was Rabbi Meir a *rodef shalom*? When have you been a *rodef shalom*?

God created the world in six days. On The seventh day God rested from the work of creation. God then made it a mitzvah that people should also rest every seventh day. The seventh day is called *Shabbat*. It is a day of study and prayer. It is a time for friends and family. Shabbat is when we rest and renew our soul.

שַׁ Shabbat

The Ox That Celebrates Shabbat

Once there was a Jewish farmer. Like all Jews he would work his farm six days a week and rest on the seventh. His family would spend six days in the field. On Shabbat they would dress up. They would eat special meals. They would go to synagogue. On Shabbat they had a day of complete rest.

This farmer had an ox. All week they worked together in the fields. The farmer and the ox plowed straight rows in the soil together. When it was planting time the ox pulled a wagon of seeds. The farmer walked alongside and took the seeds and planted in the plowed rows. At the end of the year the ox and the farmer worked together to harvest the wheat. If a man and an ox can be best friends, this man and this ox were best friends. The farmer and his ox rested on Shabbat together. Sometimes the ox and his farmer even took Shabbat walks together. They both loved to visit the stream and soak their feet on Saturday afternoon.

One year there was very little rain. Even though the ox and the farmer worked very hard, there was very little food. The family was hungry. The farmer did something he hated. He spent a whole night crying alone in his bed. Then he got up in the morning and sold his ox to his next-door neighbor, who was not a Jew. He told his neighbor, "This ox is a good worker. This ox will work as hard as you want." And he said, "This will be the best ox you will ever buy."

The new owner and the ox started to work. The neighbor saw that the ox was a very hard worker. He believed the words

of his neighbor. This was true for two or three days. Then, all of a sudden, the ox refused to leave his stall. The neighbor yelled at the ox. He hit the ox. The ox would not move. Nothing he tried could move the ox. He left the ox and went out to work. The next day the farmer got up and left the house. He saw the ox standing by the plow ready to work again. "This is strange," thought the farmer. "But it is over. I will understand it someday."

The ox continued to work hard for six days. Then all of a sudden it refused to work again. The farmer tried everything. Finally he went to his neighbor and told him the whole story. Suddenly the Jewish farmer understood. He went to the ox and patted his nose. He scratched the ox behind the ear. Then he whispered, "Brother Ox, when you were with my family you lived like a Jew. Just like my family, you rested on Shabbat. Torah tells us that Jews and their animals should rest on Shabbat. Now you are part of a non-Jewish family. Torah does

not make them observe Shabbat as we do. Please be good to your new family. I promise that as soon as I have enough money I will buy you back. We will again walk to the stream on Saturday afternoon together."

The ox got up and walked over to the wagon and stood there ready to work. The neighbor asked the Jew what had happened, and the Jew explained all. From that day on the neighbor had a great respect for the Jews and all their customs.

A Folktale

131

TO THINK ABOUT

1. God never gets tired. Why did God rest on the seventh day?

2. Why did the Jewish farmer let his ox rest on Shabbat?

3. What did the non–Jewish neighbor learn from the Jew and his ox?

שִׂמְחָה Simhah

God wants us to be happy. God makes joy a *mitzvah*. *Simhah* is the Hebrew word for "joy." A *simhah* is a special moment of happiness. A *simhah* is a time when we gather family and friends together. Joy comes from doing things well. Joy comes from following the *mitzvot*. Joy also comes from family and friends. And joy comes from knowing that God created us and the world we live in.

It Is Time to Dance

It was a wedding party. Everyone was happy. It was a real *simḥah*. Everyone wanted to make sure that the bride and groom had the best time. Everyone wanted to fulfill the *mitzvah* of rejoicing with the bride and groom.

Then the old man limped in on his cane. It was hard for him to walk. Every step was painful. He walked into the room, and the young folks brought the chair to him. They made him comfortable. The dancing went on. The old man sat in his chair holding his cane. When you looked at the old man's face you saw a wonderful smile. His eyes never left the dancers.

The band played for hours. The dancing went on. Then the band stopped for a rest. It got quiet. The old man said, "I want to tell a story." Two men picked up his chair and put him on the stage. Everyone gathered around.

The old man began, "Once there was a time when the winter was very cold. It was a time when many Jews were hungry. Rabbi Uri began collecting *tzedakah*. He went from street to street. He went from town to town. Rabbi Uri collected a lot of money—but not enough money. He came to Rabbi Moshe Lev and asked for help. Rabbi Moshe Lev asked Rabbi Uri to sit down. Much to his surprise, Rabbi Lev began to dance and dance. Rabbi Uri sat. Rabbi Moshe Lev danced and danced. When he finally stopped, Rabbi Uri said, "That was very lovely

dancing." Then he said, "But I need your help collecting money."

Rabbi Moshe Lev said, "Wait for me here."

Moshe Lev left and was gone for two days. Rabbi Uri was really angry. Rabbi Moshe Lev said, "I am very sorry, my friend. I had no choice. Here is what happened.

When I was young the Russians put an old rabbi in jail. We needed a lot of money to ransom him. They gave me a young boy to be my guide. We went from door to door. We went from street to street. Just because of this boy, I easily collected the money very quickly. I promised him that I would dance at his wedding.

"I left you to collect your money. I took ten steps and heard music. I followed the music to a wedding. It was the wedding of that very boy. I kept my promise. I have been dancing for the past two days."

Rabbi Uri was angry. He said, "But what about the money I need? How could you forget? You promised."

Rabbi Moshe Lev smiled. He reached into his pocket and pulled out a big sack of coins. He turned to Rabbi Uri and said, "A little dancing can solve just about everything."

At the wedding everyone was listening to the old man's story. As he told it he seemed to get younger and younger. Halfway through it he used his cane to push himself to his feet. When he reached the end of the story he was light on his feet. He was actually dancing when he said, "A little dancing can solve just about everything."

A Hasidic Story

TO THINK ABOUT

1. Why would God make it a *mitzvah* to be happy?

2. Where do you think Rabbi Moshe Lev got the money that Rabbi Uri needed?

3. How do you think that old man was able to dance?

Talmud Torah

God gave Israel the Torah at Mount Sinai. It was an amazing moment. The mountain shook. There was thunder and lightning. God's voice boomed from the top of the mountain. Every Jew heard the whisper of God speaking in his or her own ears. Together all of the Families-of-Israel shouted, "We will do and we will listen."

When we study Torah we can have a Mount Sinai moment. The *mitzvah* to study is called *Talmud Torah*.

The Light of Torah

This Pasha was a mean man. He thought he was the king of the little town of Tzfat. He wanted to be the boss over everyone.

This Pasha was happiest when everyone was scared of him.

Tzfat is a little town in the north of Israel. It is built on top of a mountain and has a beautiful view. This story happened long ago. It was a time when not that many Jews lived in the Land of Israel. It was a time when only some of the people in Tzfat were Jewish. Most of the people were not Jewish. The Pasha was mean to everyone, but he was especially mean to the Jews. He made many laws that made everyone unhappy. The latest law was this: "Jewish children are not allowed to study Torah."

Jews had lived in Tzfat for a long time. They knew this Pasha. He was no Haman. He was no Antiochus. This Pasha only wanted to make them beg. Once they begged and pleaded he would give in. He didn't want to kill anyone or put them in jail. This Pasha only wanted to feel like he was a big man. The Jews of Tzfat had an idea. Actually the Jewish children of Tzfat had the idea.

Mordechai said: "During the day all of us work. Some of us tend the sheep. Some of us work in the wool shops. Some of us help to make shoes. We only get together in the late afternoon to study after the work is done."

Sammy added: "We can wait until it is almost dark. Then we can sneak into the schoolhouse. The Pasha will never know we are there. We can study Torah together without having to beg."

Everyone liked the idea. The next day they tried it. Sammy sneaked up the hill from where he left Kelev, his dog, watching the sheep. Miriam pretended she was delivering butter. Mordechai jumped from roof to roof.

Each of the students found a different secret path. They met in the classroom to study. They had fooled the Pasha. But when they opened their books they found it was too dark to see the words. They did not dare light the lanterns. That much light the Pasha's guard would surely see.

Barukh had the next idea. Or maybe it was David. They decided to go down by the stream and collect fireflies. The fireflies would give them enough light to read. The light from the fireflies would not be bright enough for the Pasha's guard to see. The next night the children brought hundreds of fireflies in boxes. They opened the boxes and started to study.

The guard reported a strange glow in the school. The Pasha rushed up the hill to see what was there. He looked through the window. He saw a strange sight. Children were sitting at their desks. Their holy books were open. And circling the head of every child were hundreds of fireflies. The flies did not fly away. They did not leave. The fireflies glittered and blinked and gave enough light for each child to read the holy words.

The next day the Pasha changed his rule. Jewish study and Jewish prayer were now legal again. From time to time the Pasha even came and sat in the back of the classroom and listened to the lesson. He used to say, "I know how to make people do what I want—but I do not know how to control nature." And when he said that, one of the students would always correct him. "It was not the light of nature that helped us, it was the light of the Torah. That light will never go out."

TO THINK ABOUT

1. What was the latest rule the Pasha made?

2. Why was it important to the Jewish children to keep studying Torah?

3. Was this a miracle?

Tikkun Olam

God needs our help. God needs us to be partners. The world is not perfect. Some things are broken. Some things are not finished. People are hungry or homeless. There is not justice for all. Some people are still slaves or still treated badly. It is our job to help God finish the world and make it perfect. We have to be the arms and legs that do the work. We need to be the mouths and hearts that teach the lessons. The job of finishing the work that God started is called *tikkun olam*.

The Jewel

This jewel was the biggest and the best of all the jewels that came out of the mine. The king wanted it from the minute he saw it. It was the best. He had to have it. He said, "If it is the best, if it is the biggest, it is mine!"

The king first saw the jewel when he was visiting his ruby mine. He saw it lying in a wagon of unpolished stones. He picked it up. He put it in his pocket. He said "Mine" and walked out of the mine. He knew it was the biggest. He knew it was the best. The king didn't need to see anything else.

The king gave the giant ruby to the royal jeweler. He said to him, "Polish it. Make it perfect." The jeweler put the ocular in his eye. He looked at every side of the ruby. He looked over and over again. Finally, in a soft and shaky voice, he said, "Your majesty, there is a crack in this stone."

The king said, "So fix it."

The jeweler said, "I am sorry, your majesty, but it cannot be done."

The king went and got another royal jeweler. This one put in his ocular. This one also looked and looked. After a long time this one said, "Your majesty, the best thing we can do is cut the big stone into three beautiful smaller stones. Each one of the three will be wonderful."

The king said, "Then it will not be the biggest. Then it will not be the best." Then the king went and got a new royal jeweler. The king got a lot of new royal jewelers because not one of them knew how to fix a crack in a large and beautiful ruby.

The king left the ruby on the table. One day a visitor came to the palace. He said, "Your majesty, may I look at your stone?" The king gave permission. He took out his ocular and looked and looked. After a long time he said, "I can make your stone into something beautiful."

The king asked, "Will it be big? Will it be beautiful? Will it be perfect?"

The visitor said, "Yes. Yes. Yes." He took the stone and went into the workshop. Everywhere in the palace you could hear the grinding and the polishing. It took three days.

The visitor came before the king with the jewel under a black cloth. The king asked, "Is it still big?" The visitor nodded. "Is it still beautiful?" The visitor nodded. "Is it perfect?" The visitor nodded. Then the king asked, "How did you get rid of the crack?"

The visitor said, "The crack is still here, Your Majesty."

The king started to say, "But, but, but, but—" when the visitor pulled the cloth off the ruby. Everyone in the palace gasped. The stone was huge. It was beautiful. At the center of the stone was now carved a wonderful rose. The crack had become the stem.

The king opened his mouth and said, "Wow." Then the king did something unusual. He stopped talking. He just looked and looked at the jewel. Later he rewarded the jeweler. He showed everyone who came to the palace his jewel with a rose. He told everyone the story of how a crack became a rose. At the end of the story the king told everyone, "I learned the most important lesson of my life that day."

Things in the kingdom were much better from that day on.

A Story of the Maggid of Dubnow

TO THINK ABOUT

1. What did the king always want?

2. What lesson did the visitor teach the king?

3. How are people like that jewel?

4. What are ways we can do *tikkun olam*? What does this story teach us about *tikkun olam*?